THE CHOCOLATE COOKBOOK

by MARCY and MICHAEL MAGER

Illustrated by Sven Lindman

SCHOLASTIC BOOK SERVICES

NEW YORK • TORONTO • LONDON • AUCKLAND • SYDNEY • TOKYO

To Claudia Lewis, for caring

ISBN: 0-590-08033-4

Copyright © 1977 by Scholastic Magazines, Inc. All rights reserved. Published by Scholastic Book Services, a division of Scholastic Inc.

12 11 10 9 8 7 6   1 2 3 4 5/8

Printed in the U.S.A.   07

THE CHOCOLATE COOKBOOK

Contents

Chocolate is probably the world's favorite food. You can drink it hot or cold, or eat it as a snack or as part of a meal. It is made into pies, cakes, cookies, candy, ice cream, and even breakfast cereal. Chocolate comes in lacy Valentine boxes and in survival kits. It is nourishing, energy-giving, and satisfying.

Chocolate came to us from Mexico — but by way of Europe. When the Spanish explorer Cortéz arrived at the court of Montezuma, the Aztec Emperor, he found him drinking a cold, bitter drink called Chocolatl. It was made from seeds of the cacao tree, ground in water and mixed with spices. Montezuma gave Cortéz the recipe and some cacao and vanilla beans. Cortéz took them back to Spain, where the Spanish king and queen quickly improved the drink by adding sugar and having it served hot.

For about a hundred years chocolate was exclusively a royal Spanish treat. But once the secret leaked out, the upper classes in most of the European capitals were soon sipping hot chocolate.

From Amsterdam, the Dutch settlers brought chocolate to the American colonies, and in 1765 a man named Baker started a chocolate mill near Boston. By this time, people had figured out how to make powdered cocoa by extracting some of the cocoa butter and adding it to the ground beans to make solid chocolate.

A hundred years later a man in Switzerland named Daniel Peter found a way to make solid sweet milk chocolate, and a great candy business was born. Chocolate companies like Nestlé and Hershey need a lot of cacao beans. About one-third of the supply — over 350 thousand tons — is imported each year from the African country of Ghana. Ghana is the world's largest supplier of cacao beans.

For many years, chocolate was made by hand; now machines do most of the work. Today, you can buy all kinds of packaged chocolate in your local supermarket, but you can still create royal, handmade chocolate treats in your own kitchen!

This book tells you how to use chocolate to make marvelous kinds of cakes, cookies, candy, and other mouth-watering delights. There are enough recipes here to keep your sweet tooth happy for years to come.

There are even some brain-teasing puzzles to do while you munch on your homemade chocolate treats.

Try one of these delicious recipes when you feel like treating yourself, your family, and your friends — and when you have plenty of time in the kitchen and there's an adult around. You can pick and choose among the recipes, but remember . . .

These recipes are super-rich, sweet, and creamy — and sometimes costly. So, like all sweets, they should be served on special occasions and eaten in small amounts. In fact, many of these recipes can be cut in half. To do this, divide *everything* by 2, and write down the new quantities before cooking.

Read through the **Safety and Cooking Tips** (p. 72) before you cook each time, until you know them. They will make your cooking experiences safe, enjoyable, and successful.

Fun and Easy

Ice Cream Soda

½ cup milk
4 tablespoons chocolate syrup (ready-made or see recipe p. 13)
1 scoop chocolate ice cream
club soda or seltzer water

❁❁❁❁❁❁

1. Mix the syrup and the milk together in a tall glass. Use a long spoon.
2. Add a little club soda or seltzer water and stir.
3. Add the ice cream.
4. Add enough club soda or seltzer water to fill the glass.
5. Stir and drink!

Chocolate Egg Cream

3 tablespoons chocolate syrup (ready-made or see recipe p. 13)
½ cup milk
club soda or seltzer water

❁❁❁❁❁❁

1. Stir the chocolate syrup and the milk together in a tall glass.
2. Add the club soda or seltzer water very slowly and stir with a long spoon, to make a smooth fine foam on top. Then *drink it*!

The original egg cream was made with cream and egg. The modern egg cream is light, delicious, and foamy too. Some people will travel miles to get a perfect egg cream.

Super Shakes

2 cups very cold milk
6 tablespoons chocolate syrup (ready-made or see recipe p. 13)
2 scoops chocolate or vanilla ice cream

❈❈❈❈❈❈

1. Beat the milk, syrup, and ice cream together in a small mixing bowl. Use an egg-beater.
2. Pour into two tall glasses.
3. Top with whipped cream and sprinkle lightly with ground nutmeg, cinnamon, or cloves.

Marvelous Malts

Add 4 tablespoons of malted milk powder and one more scoop of ice cream to the ingredients for the Super Shake. Beat together and serve according to that recipe.

Whipped Cream

½ pint heavy cream
2 tablespoons sifted confectioners' sugar
½ teaspoon vanilla extract

❈❈❈❈❈❈

1. Chill the cream, a medium-sized mixing bowl, and the beaters of an electric mixer in the refrigerator.
2. Pour the chilled heavy cream into the chilled bowl.
3. Set the electric mixer on high speed to beat the cream. **Do not use a blender.** The cream will take about 4 minutes to thicken.
4. **Do not overbeat.** The whipped cream is ready if it stands in "peaks" when the beater blades are lifted out of the mixture. **Turn off the mixer to test.**
5. Stir in the sugar and vanilla.

Make whipped cream just before you want to use it.

11

Hot Cocoa for One

1 tablespoon cocoa
2 tablespoons granulated sugar
1 tablespoon milk
1 cup milk or water — or a mixture of half milk, half water (whichever you prefer)

∞●∞●∞●∞●∞

1. Mix the cocoa and the sugar in a mug.
2. Add the tablespoon of milk. Stir until you have a smooth paste.
3. Heat the cup of milk or water over low heat in a small saucepan. **Do not boil**. Turn off the stove.
4. Pour the hot milk or water over the cocoa mixture in the mug. Stir well.

If you don't like very sweet cocoa, use only 1 tablespoon of sugar in this recipe and ⅔ cup of sugar in the cocoa recipe for 8. You can always add sugar later.

Hot Cocoa for a Party
Serves 8

½ cup cocoa
1 cup granulated sugar
½ cup milk
2 quarts milk or water — or a mixture of milk and water
½ tablespoon vanilla or peppermint extract
8 large marshmallows

∞●∞●∞●∞●∞

1. Mix the cocoa, sugar, and the ½ cup of milk in a large saucepan.
2. Pour in the 2 quarts of milk or water. Mix with a long spoon.
3. Set the saucepan over low heat and stir constantly. **Do not boil**.
4. Turn off the stove, remove saucepan to sink, and stir in the extract.
5. With a cup, dip the cocoa out of the saucepan into the mugs. Add a marshmallow or some whipped cream (see p. 11) to each mug.

Best Chocolate Syrup
Makes 1½ cups

4 squares unsweetened chocolate
¾ cup boiling water
1¼ cups granulated sugar
½ teaspoon vanilla extract

1. Melt the chocolate squares in the top of a double boiler over hot, **but not boiling,** water. (Stove should be at lowest setting.) Stir occasionally with a long spoon.
2. Pour 1 cup of water into a small saucepan. Set the saucepan on medium heat. Bring the water to a boil.
3. Carefully measure ¾ cup of the boiling water into a plastic measuring cup.
4. Add the boiling water to the melted chocolate. Stir well.
5. Add the sugar to the chocolate, a little at a time, and stir.
6. Cook the chocolate mixture for 5 minutes, stirring constantly.
7. Turn off the stove. **Carefully** lift off the top of the double boiler and set it aside. Let the chocolate syrup cool for a few minutes.
8. Add the vanilla and stir.
9. Use the syrup right away, or pour it into a container and let it cool.
10. Cover it tightly, and store it in the refrigerator until needed. The syrup will stay fresh for a few weeks.

Hot Fudge Sauce

Makes 1 cup

2 squares unsweetened chocolate
⅓ cup boiling water
1 tablespoon butter or margarine

½ cup light corn syrup
¼ cup granulated sugar
½ teaspoon vanilla extract

1. Melt the chocolate squares in the top of a double boiler over hot, **but not boiling,** water. (Stove should be at lowest setting.) Stir occasionally with a long spoon.
2. Pour 1 cup of water into a small saucepan. Set the saucepan on medium heat. Bring the water to a boil.
3. When the chocolate is melted, turn off the stove and **carefully** lift off the top of the double boiler.
4. Carefully measure ⅓ cup of the boiling water into a plastic measuring cup.
5. Add the boiling water and the butter or margarine to the chocolate. Mix well.
6. Place the top of the double boiler directly over low heat. Bring the mixture to a boil, slowly, stirring all the time with a long spoon.
7. When the chocolate mixture comes to a boil, add the corn syrup and boil for 4 minutes. Continue stirring.
8. Add the sugar and boil for 3 more minutes, stirring all the time.
9. Turn off the stove and set the pot aside to cool for a few minutes.
10. Add the vanilla and stir.
11. Use as is, or chill for 1 hour in the refrigerator to get a thicker sauce. Use over plain cake, ice cream, or puddings.

Mint Fudge Sauce

Makes 1 cup

2 squares unsweetened chocolate
1 tablespoon butter or margarine
⅓ cup milk

½ cup light corn syrup
⅓ cup granulated sugar
1 teaspoon peppermint extract

1. Drop the chocolate in the top of a double boiler and melt it over hot, **but not boiling,** water. (Stove at lowest setting.) Stir occasionally with a long spoon.
2. Add the butter or margarine and stir.
3. Add the milk.
4. **Carefully** lift off the top of the double boiler and place it directly over the heat. Bring the mixture to a boil slowly, stirring all the time.
5. When the chocolate mixture comes to a boil, add the corn syrup and boil for 3 minutes. Continue stirring.
6. Add the sugar and boil for 3 more minutes, stirring all the time.
7. Turn off the stove and set the pot aside to cool for a few minutes.
8. Add the peppermint extract and stir.
9. Serve hot or cold over plain cake, ice cream, or puddings. Tightly cover the sauce when you store it in the refrigerator.

You can vary this sauce by using another **extract** — almond **or** lemon **or** orange — instead of peppermint.

Creamy Chocolate Sauce
Makes 1 cup

2 squares semi-sweet chocolate
2 tablespoons butter or margarine
1 cup granulated sugar
¼ cup milk
¼ cup cold water
1 teaspoon vanilla extract

1. Melt the chocolate and the butter or margarine in the top of a double boiler over low heat. **Do not boil.**
2. As the chocolate melts, stir in the sugar, milk, and water. Use a long spoon.
3. Cook the sauce until it is as thick as you want it. Keep stirring as it cooks.
4. Turn off the stove and **carefully** lift off the top of the double boiler. Let cool for a few minutes, then add the vanilla and stir.
5. Serve hot or cold over plain cake, ice cream, or puddings.

Cocoa Nut-Squares

Makes about 40 squarss

⅓ cup butter or margarine
⅔ cup light corn syrup
2 teaspoons almond extract
¾ cup cocoa
1¼ cups confectioners' sugar
1½ cups chopped unsalted nuts
¾ cup shredded coconut
2 cups rice cereal, such as Rice Krispies
2 cups toasted oat cereal, such as Cheerios

1. Grease a 13x9-inch cake pan (see p. 75).
2. Melt the butter or margarine in a small saucepan over low heat, then pour it into a large bowl.
3. Add the corn syrup, almond extract, and cocoa. Mix well.
4. Sift the sugar into the mixture in the bowl. Mix.
5. Add the nuts, coconut, and cereals. Mix well after you add each. Use a fork at first, then a spoon.
6. With the spoon, push the mixture into the greased pan. Press it down with the fork.
7. Put the pan in the refrigerator until the mixture is firm — about 2 or 3 hours.
8. To serve, cut in 1½ inch squares, and lift out carefully.

Peanut Nibblers
Makes about 48 nibblers

1 cup semi-sweet chocolate chips
½ cup peanut butter
2 cups cornflakes
½ cup quick-cooking rolled oats
½ cup shredded coconut

½ cup light corn syrup
1 teaspoon vanilla extract
⅓ cup chopped, unsalted peanuts
48 unchopped peanuts for decoration

1. Cover a cookie sheet with waxed paper.
2. Mix the peanut butter, cornflakes, rolled oats, and coconut together in a large bowl.
3. Drop the chocolate chips in the top of a double boiler and melt them over hot, **but not boiling,** water. (Stove at lowest setting.) Stir occasionally with a long spoon.
4. When the chocolate is melted, turn off the stove and **carefully** lift off the top of the double boiler. Let chocolate cool for a minute.
5. Add the cornflake mixture to the chocolate in the top of the double boiler. Stir until well mixed.
6. Add the corn syrup, vanilla, and chopped nuts. Stir again.
7. Drop the mixture, by rounded teaspoonfuls, on the prepared cookie sheet. Use a regular teaspoon, not a measuring spoon. Top each nibbler with a whole nut.
8. Put the cookie sheet in the refrigerator until the mixture is firm. This will take about 2 hours.

Chocolate Crisps

Makes about 30 crisps

1½ cups milk-chocolate chips
2 cups rice cereal, such as Rice Krispies
⅔ cup miniature marshmallows
1½ teaspoons almond extract
½ cup chopped unsalted nuts
⅓ cup raisins

1. Cover a cookie sheet with waxed paper.
2. Drop the chocolate in the top of a double boiler and melt it over hot, **but not boiling**, water. (Stove at lowest setting.) Stir occasionally with a long spoon.
3. When the chocolate is melted, turn off the stove and **carefully** lift off the top of the double boiler. Let chocolate cool for a minute.
4. Add the cereal and the marshmallows to the chocolate in the top of the double boiler. Mix well.
5. Add the almond extract, nuts, and raisins to the chocolate mixture. Stir well.
6. Wash and dry your hands. Then, with your fingers, shape the mixture into balls about the size of walnuts. Place them on the prepared cookie sheet.
7. Put the cookie sheet in the refrigerator until the mixture is firm. This will take about 2 or 3 hours.

Cookies and Brownies

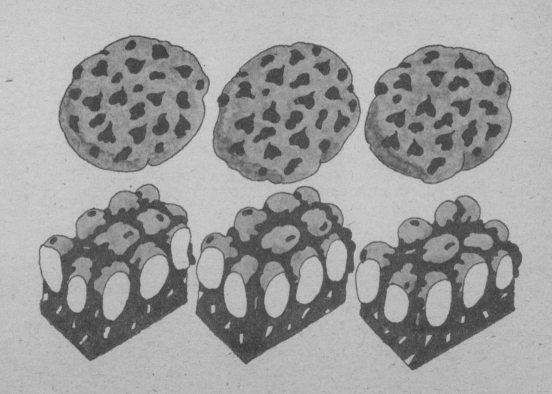

Coco-Nutters

Makes about 40 cookies

4 squares unsweetened chocolate
2 cups condensed milk
¼ teaspoon salt
8 ounces shredded coconut

1⅓ cups chopped walnuts (or another kind of unsalted nut if you prefer)
1 teaspoon vanilla extract

1. Set the oven to 375 degrees.
2. Tear off enough waxed paper to cover a cookie sheet. Grease the cookie sheet *and* the waxed paper. Put the waxed paper over the cookie sheet, greased side up.
3. Drop the chocolate in the top of a double boiler and melt it over hot, **but not boiling,** water. (Stove at lowest setting.) Stir occasionally with a long spoon.
4. When the chocolate is melted, turn off the stove and **carefully** lift off the top of the double boiler. Let chocolate cool for a minute.
5. Add the milk, salt, coconut, nuts, and vanilla to the chocolate in the top of the double boiler. Stir well.
6. Drop the mixture, by teaspoonfuls, onto the prepared cookie sheet. Use a regular teaspoon, not a measuring spoon. Leave some room around each cookie. They will spread out.
7. Bake about 8 minutes.
8. Let the cookies cool for 5 or 10 minutes on the waxed paper before you try to remove them. The cookies will be a little sticky. Arrange them on a plate when cool.

Peanut Delights

Makes about 50 cookies

¼ cup butter or margarine
⅔ cup peanut butter
½ cup granulated sugar
½ cup brown sugar
1¼ cups all-purpose flour
½ teaspoon salt

½ teaspoon baking soda
1 teaspoon vanilla extract
1 egg
½ cup semi-sweet chocolate chips
¼ cup chopped unsalted peanuts

1. Set the oven to 375 degrees.
2. Grease a large cookie sheet (see p. 75).
3. Stir the butter or margarine and the peanut butter together in a large bowl. Mix well. Use a fork.
4. Add the granulated sugar and the brown sugar to the peanut butter mixture and stir well with a mixing spoon.
5. Sift in the flour, salt, and baking soda. Mix well.
6. Add the vanilla.
7. Break the egg into a cup (see p. 74), then add to mixture in the bowl. Mix well.
8. Add the chocolate chips and nuts. Mix well. Mixture will be thick, almost stiff.
9. Drop the mixture, by teaspoonfuls, on the prepared cookie sheet. Leave about 2 inches between each cookie. Press the cookies down with the back of the spoon.
10. Bake about 8 minutes. Let cool for 5 minutes before removing cookies from pan to plate with a spatula.

Chocolate Pecan Drops

Makes about 30 cookies

3 squares semi-sweet chocolate
2 tablespoons milk
⅔ cup butter or margarine
½ teaspoon salt
½ cup granulated sugar

1 tablespoon vanilla extract
1¼ cups all-purpose flour
¾ cup chopped pecans (or whatever kind of unsalted nut you like)
granulated sugar for rolling

1. Set oven to 375 degrees
2. Melt the chocolate in the top of a double boiler over hot, **not boiling,** water. (Stove at lowest setting.) Add the milk and stir occasionally with a long spoon.
3. When the chocolate is melted, turn off the stove and **carefully** lift off the top of the double boiler. Set chocolate aside to cool.
4. Mix the butter or margarine, the salt, and sugar in a large bowl. Beat with a mixing spoon until creamy.
5. Add the vanilla and the cooled chocolate to the butter mixture. Mix well.
6. Sift in the flour. Mix again.
7. Add the pecans and mix. The mixture will be quite thick.
8. Wash and dry your hands. Then, with your fingers, shape the mixture into balls about the size of walnuts.
9. Pour enough granulated sugar into a saucer to cover the bottom of the dish. Roll the balls in the sugar. Add more sugar to the saucer as needed.
10. Place balls on an **ungreased** cookie sheet.
11. Bake for 15 to 20 minutes. Let cool for 5 minutes before removing cookies from pan to plate with a spatula.

Chocolate Chip Oatmeal Cookies

Makes about 40 cookies

½ cup canned shortening, such as Crisco
⅓ cup brown sugar
⅓ cup granulated sugar
¾ teaspoon vanilla extract
1 egg
¾ cup all-purpose flour
½ teaspoon salt

1 teaspoon baking powder
⅓ cup milk
1¾ cups quick-cooking rolled oats
⅓ cup chopped walnuts
⅓ cup raisins
1 cup milk-chocolate chips

1. Set the oven to 375 degrees.
2. Grease a cookie sheet.
3. Mix the shortening, brown sugar, and granulated sugar in a large bowl. Beat with a mixing spoon until creamy.
4. Break the egg into a cup (see p. 74). Add the vanilla to the egg and mix with a fork. Add the egg mixture to the shortening mixture.
5. Sift the flour, salt, and baking powder together into another large bowl.
6. Add a tablespoon of the flour mixture, then a little milk, to the shortening mixture. Stir. Repeat until all the flour mixture and milk have been added.
7. Add the rolled oats. Mix well.
8. Add the nuts, then the raisins, then the chocolate chips. Mix well after you add each. The mixture will be very thick.
9. Drop the mixture, by teaspoonfuls, on the prepared cookie sheet. Leave plenty of room around each cookie. They will spread out.
10. Bake about 12 minutes. Let cool for 5 minutes before removing cookies from pan to plate with a spatula.

Spicy Chip Cookies
Makes about 35 cookies

1 cup all-purpose flour
½ teaspoon salt
½ teaspoon baking soda
½ teaspoon cinnamon
½ teaspoon nutmeg
½ cup of butter or other soft shortening

⅓ cup granulated sugar
½ cup brown sugar
½ teaspoon vanilla extract
1 egg
1 cup semi-sweet chocolate chips
½ cup chopped unsalted nuts

1. Set the oven to 375 degrees.
2. Grease a large cookie sheet.
3. Sift the flour, salt, baking soda, cinnamon, and nutmeg into a large bowl.
4. In another large bowl, mix the shortening, the granulated sugar, the brown sugar, and the vanilla. Stir until well mixed.
5. Break the egg into a cup (see p. 74), then add it to the shortening mixture. Beat until the mixture is fluffy. Use a mixing spoon.
6. Add the flour mixture to the shortening mixture. Mix well.
7. Add the nuts and chocolate chips. Stir slowly. The mixture will be thick.
8. Drop the mixture, by teaspoonfuls, on the prepared cookie sheet. Leave plenty of room around each cookie. They will spread out.
9. Bake about 13 minutes. Let cool for 5 minutes before removing cookies from pan to plate with a spatula.

Marshmallow Nut Brownies

Makes 16 brownies

2 squares unsweetened chocolate
⅓ cup butter or margarine
¾ cup all-purpose flour
½ teaspoon baking powder
¼ teaspoon salt

1 cup granulated sugar
2 eggs
1 teaspoon vanilla extract
⅓ cup chopped walnuts
¼ cup miniature marshmallows

1. Set the oven to 350 degrees.
2. Grease an 8-inch-square cake pan.
3. Melt the chocolate and the butter or margarine in the top of a double boiler over hot, **but not boiling**, water. (Stove at lowest setting.) Stir with a long spoon while the chocolate melts.
4. When the chocolate is melted, turn off the stove. **Carefully** lift off the top of the double boiler. Set chocolate aside to cool.
5. Sift flour, salt, and baking powder into a large bowl. Set aside.
6. Break the eggs into another large bowl (see p. 74). Beat them with a mixing spoon until frothy.
7. Beat the sugar into the eggs, a little at a time.
8. Add the chocolate mixture and the vanilla to the egg mixture. Stir well.
9. Stir the flour mixture into the egg mixture.
10. Add nuts and marshmallows. Stir well.
11. Pour into prepared pan. Spread evenly with the back of the spoon.
12. Bake for 30 minutes. Let brownies cool in the pan for 10 to 15 minutes before you cut them into 2-inch squares. Then remove them with a spatula to a cake rack.

Coconut Brownies
Makes 16 brownies

2 squares unsweetened chocolate
⅓ cup butter or margarine
¾ cup all-purpose flour
½ teaspoon baking powder
¼ teaspoon salt
1 cup granulated sugar
2 eggs
1 teaspoon vanilla extract
¾ cup shredded coconut
⅓ cup chopped walnuts

◦●◦●◦●◦●◦

Follow cooking directions for Marshmallow Nut Brownies, but substitute the coconut for the marshmallows in step 10. When baked and cut, sprinkle with confectioners' sugar.

Frosty Mint Brownies
Makes 16 brownies

2 squares unsweetened chocolate
⅓ cup butter or margarine
¾ cup all-purpose flour
½ teaspoon baking powder
¼ teaspoon salt
1 cup granulated sugar
2 eggs
1½ teaspoons peppermint extract
½ cup walnuts or ½ cup raisins — or use ¼ cup of each

◦●◦●◦●◦●◦

Follow cooking directions for Marshmallow Nut Brownies, but substitute the raisins for the marshmallows in step 10.

Cupcakes, Cakes, and Frostings

Real Chocolate Cupcakes

Makes about 30 cupcakes

½ cup butter or margarine
1½ cups granulated sugar
2 eggs
1¾ cups all-purpose flour
½ cup cocoa
1 teaspoon baking soda

½ teaspoon baking powder
½ teaspoon salt
1 cup milk
1 teaspoon vanilla extract
½ cup semi-sweet chocolate chips

1. Set the oven to 350 degrees.
2. Prepare cupcake pans by greasing and flouring each cup thoroughly. Or put a paper cupcake liner in each cup.
3. Mix the butter or margarine and the sugar in a large bowl. Beat with a mixing spoon until smooth and creamy.
4. Break the eggs into a small bowl (see p. 74), then add them to the sugar mixture. Beat with the mixing spoon until fluffy.
5. Sift the flour, cocoa, baking soda, baking powder, and salt into another large bowl.
6. Add the milk to the flour mixture, a little at a time, and mix well.
7. Add the egg mixture to the flour mixture and mix well.
8. Add the vanilla and the chocolate chips. Stir thoroughly.
9. Fill each cupcake cup half full by dipping a regular cup into the batter, and pouring the batter into the cupcake cups.
10. Bake about 20 minutes. Let the cupcakes cool in the pan for 10 minutes before you remove them to a cake rack.
11. When the cupcakes are thoroughly cool, frost them with Plain Old Chocolate Frosting (see p. 38).

Fudge Nut Cake

2 squares unsweetened chocolate
1 cup cake flour
½ teaspoon salt
½ teaspoon baking soda
½ cup butter or other soft shortening
1 cup granulated sugar
1 egg
1 teaspoon almond extract
½ cup milk
¾ cup chopped walnuts

1. Set the oven to 350 degrees.
2. Grease and flour an 8-inch-square cake pan (see p. 75).
3. Drop the chocolate in the top of a double boiler and melt it over hot, **but not boiling,** water. (Stove at lowest setting.) Stir occasionally with a long spoon.

4. When the chocolate is melted, turn off the stove and **carefully** lift off the top of the double boiler. Set chocolate aside to cool.
5. Sift the flour, salt, and baking soda into a large bowl. Set the bowl aside.
6. In another large bowl, beat the sugar and the shortening with a mixing spoon until smooth and creamy.
7. Break the egg into a cup (see p. 74), then add it to the shortening mixture. Beat until fluffy.
8. Add the cooled chocolate and almond extract to the shortening mixture. Mix well.
9. Add a tablespoon of the flour mixture, then a little milk, to the shortening mixture. Stir. Repeat until all the flour mixture and milk have been added.
10. Add the nuts and stir.
11. Pour into prepared pan.
12. Bake for 35 to 40 minutes, then test for doneness (see page 76).
13. Let the cake cool in the pan for 10 to 15 minutes. Then turn it out on a cake rack (see page 76).
14. Frost the top with Coconut Almond Frosting (use half the recipe on p. 40). You can also sprinkle with chopped nuts.

Devil's Delight Layer Cake

2 squares unsweetened chocolate
1¾ cups cake flour
½ teaspoon salt
1 teaspoon baking soda
¾ cup brown sugar

⅔ cup granulated sugar
½ cup butter or other soft shortening
2 eggs
¾ cup milk
1 teaspoon vanilla extract

1. Set the oven to 350 degrees.
2. Grease and flour 2 square 8-inch cake pans.

3. Melt the chocolate in the top of a double boiler over hot, **but not boiling,** water. (Stove at lowest setting.) Stir occasionally with a long spoon.

4. When the chocolate is melted, turn off the stove and **carefully** lift off the top of the double boiler. Set chocolate aside to cool.
5. Sift the flour, baking soda, and salt into a large bowl. Set the bowl aside.
6. In another large bowl, mix the brown sugar, granulated sugar, and shortening. Beat with a mixing spoon until smooth and creamy.
7. Break the eggs into a cup (see p. 74), then add them to the shortening mixture. Mix well.
8. Add the melted chocolate and *half* the flour mixture to the shortening mixture. Mix well.
9. Add the milk and the rest of the flour mixture to the shortening mixture. Mix again.
10. Add the vanilla. Stir.
11. Pour into prepared pans. Bake 30 minutes, then test for doneness (see p. 76).
12. Let the layers cool in the pans for 10 to 15 minutes, then turn them out on a cake rack (see p. 76).
13. When the layers are cool, put one layer on a large plate and frost it. Put the second layer on top and frost that layer. (No need to frost the sides.) You can use Chocolate Butter Mint Frosting (double the recipe on p. 39). Or use a chocolate glaze (p. 41).

Marble Spice Wonder Cake

  2 squares unsweetened chocolate
  2 cups granulated sugar
 ⅔ cup butter or other soft shortening
  2 teaspoons vanilla extract
2¼ cups cake flour
  1 teaspoon baking powder
  1 teaspoon baking soda
  1 teaspoon ginger
  1 teaspoon cinnamon
 ½ teaspoon nutmeg
 ¼ teaspoon ground cloves
  3 eggs
 ¾ cup milk

Marble cake makes a fine snacking cake with just confectioners' sugar sprinkled over the top. If you do this, drop teaspoonfuls of the sugar through a strainer to coat the cake evenly.

1. Set the oven to 350 degrees.
2. Grease and flour a 13x9-inch cake pan.
3. Drop the chocolate in the top of a double boiler and melt it over hot, **but not boiling,** water. (Stove at lowest setting.) Stir occasionally with a long spoon.
4. When the chocolate is melted, turn off the stove and **carefully** lift off the top of the double boiler. Set chocolate aside to cool.
5. Mix the sugar and the shortening in a large bowl. Use a mixing spoon and beat until smooth and creamy.
6. Add the vanilla and mix.
7. In another large bowl, sift together the flour, baking powder, baking soda, ginger, cinnamon, nutmeg, and cloves.
8. Add *some* of the flour mixture and *some* of the milk to the shortening mixture. Stir. Repeat until all the flour mixture and the milk have been added to the batter.
9. Separate the eggs (see p. 74). Mix the yolks into the batter.
10. Beat the egg whites in a separate bowl with an electric mixer (see p. 74) until they are stiff, and fold them into the batter (see p. 75).
11. Dip out 1 cup of the batter and put it in another bowl. Add the cooled chocolate to this cup of batter, mix well, and set aside.
12. Pour the rest of the batter into the pan. Dot the top with teaspoonfuls of the chocolate batter. Stir *very slowly,* just enough to streak the white batter with chocolate.
13. Bake 40 minutes, then test for doneness (see p. 76).
14. Let the cake cool for 10 to 15 minutes, then turn it out on a cake rack (see p. 76).
15. Cover the top with a chocolate glaze (see p. 41), or Plain Old Chocolate Frosting (see p. 38).

Chocolate Cream Layer Cake

3 squares unsweetened chocolate
¼ cup hot tap water
2 cups cake flour
1 teaspoon baking powder
½ teaspoon salt
1 cup butter or another soft shortening
2 cups granulated sugar
2 eggs
2 teaspoons vanilla extract
¾ cup buttermilk

For special occasions, you can serve this delicious frosted layer cake with whipped cream (see p. 11). Serve each wedge on its side on the plate, and plop a generous glob of whipped cream over it. Or you can use whipped cream for frosting the layers. Do this shortly before you serve the cake, and then chill the cake (and store it later) in the refrigerator.

1. Set the oven to 350 degrees.
2. Grease and flour 2 round 9-inch cake pans.
3. Mix the chocolate and the ¼ cup hot water in the top of a double boiler. Melt over hot, **but not boiling**, water. (Stove at lowest setting.) Stir occasionally with a long spoon.
4. When the chocolate is melted, turn off the stove and **carefully** lift off the top of the double boiler. Set chocolate aside to cool.
5. Sift the flour, baking powder, and salt into a large bowl. Set aside.
6. In another large bowl, beat the sugar and the shortening with a mixing spoon until creamy.
7. Separate the eggs (see p. 74). Add the yolks to the shortening mixture.
8. Add the vanilla. Mix.
9. Add the cooled chocolate. Mix well.
10. Add *some* of the flour mixture and *some* of the buttermilk to the shortening mixture. Beat with a mixing spoon until smooth. Repeat until all the flour mixture and all the buttermilk have been added to the batter.
11. Beat the egg whites with an electric mixer until they are stiff (see p. 74).
12. Fold the beaten egg whites into the batter (see p. 75).
13. Pour into prepared pans.
14. Bake for 40-45 minutes. Test for doneness (see p. 76).
15. Let the layers cool in the pans for 10 to 15 minutes, then turn them out on a cake rack (see p. 76).
16. When the layers are cool, put one layer on a large plate, frost it, put the second layer on top, and frost that layer. (No need to frost the sides.) You can use Plain Old Chocolate Frosting (see p. 38).

Plain Old Chocolate Frosting

Frosts two 9-inch cake layers

4 squares unsweetened chocolate
1 cup sifted confectioners' sugar
3 tablespoons hot tap water
1 egg
4 tablespoons butter or margarine

1. Drop the chocolate in the top of a double boiler and melt it over hot, **but not boiling**, water. (Stove at lowest setting.) Stir occasionally with a long spoon.
2. When the chocolate is melted, turn off the stove and **carefully** lift off the top of the double boiler. Let chocolate cool for a minute.
3. Add the sugar and 3 tablespoons of hot water to the melted chocolate. Beat with a mixing spoon.
4. Break the egg into a cup (see p. 74) and mix it with a fork. Then add it to the chocolate mixture. Beat well.
5. Add the butter or margarine, a tablespoon at a time, and beat until the frosting is smooth and creamy.
6. Spread on cake that has cooled.

Chocolate Butter Mint Frosting

Frosts one pan of brownies

1 square unsweetened chocolate
1½ cups confectioners' sugar
¼ cup butter or margarine
a dash salt
¾ teaspoon peppermint extract

●○●○●○●○●○●○●○●○●○●○●○

1. Drop the chocolate in the top of a double boiler and melt it over hot, **but not boiling**, water. (Stove at lowest setting.) Stir occasionally with a long spoon.
2. When the chocolate is melted, turn off the stove and **carefully** lift off the top of the double boiler. Set chocolate aside to cool.
3. Sift the confectioners' sugar into a large bowl.
4. In another bowl, mix the butter or margarine and the salt with ½ cup of the sifted sugar. Use a spoon and mix until light and fluffy.
5. Add a little more sugar and some of the melted chocolate to the shortening mixture. Mix well. Repeat until all the sugar and all the chocolate have been added.
6. Add the extract. Beat well with the spoon until the frosting is smooth.
7. Spread on cake that has cooled.

Coconut Almond Frosting
Frosts two 9-inch cake layers

4 squares semi-sweet chocolate
2 eggs
½ cup butter or margarine
½ teaspoon almond extract
⅓ cup shredded coconut
⅓ cup slivered or chopped almonds

1. Drop the chocolate in the top of a double boiler and melt it over hot, **but not boiling**, water. (Stove at lowest setting.) Stir occasionally with a long spoon.
2. When the chocolate is melted, turn off the stove and **carefully** lift off the top of the double boiler. Set chocolate aside to cool.
3. Break the eggs into a large bowl (see p. 74). Add the butter or margarine and mix well. Use a mixing spoon.
4. Add the chocolate to the egg mixture. Beat with the spoon until smooth.
5. Add the almond extract and stir.
6. Add the coconut and chopped almonds. Mix well.
7. Spread on cake that has cooled. You can also sprinkle a little coconut and chopped almonds on top of this frosting.

Chocolate Glazes
Frosts two 8-inch cake layers

#1

1. Melt 3 squares of semi-sweet chocolate in the top of a double boiler over hot, **but not boiling**, water. (Stove at lowest setting.)
2. When melted, add 3 teaspoons of corn syrup and 3 tablespoons of cold tap water.
3. Mix with a long spoon, then turn off the stove. Let cool for a few minutes before using.
4. Spread warm glaze over the top of the cake. Let a little glaze drip down the sides of the cake.

#2

1. Melt 4 squares of semi-sweet chocolate in the top of a double boiler over hot, **but not boiling**, water.
2. As the chocolate melts, add ¼ cup of milk. Mix well with a long spoon, then turn off the stove. Spread over cake immediately.

#3

1. Melt 3 squares of semi-sweet chocolate in the top of a double boiler over hot, **but not boiling**, water.
2. Turn off stove, and **carefully** lift off the top of the double boiler.
3. Let the pot cool for a few minutes, then add:
   - ½ teaspoon of vanilla
   - 1 tablespoon of butter or margarine
   - ⅓ cup sifted confectioners' sugar, and stir.
4. Add 1 tablespoon cold water.
5. Stir and use on cake immediately.

These glazes will thicken if they are stored in the refrigerator. They will have to be reheated in a double boiler before you can use them again.

Glaze #3 turns into candy after a few hours in the refrigerator (see p. 48).

Pancakes, Pie, and Muffins

Chocolate Pancakes

For breakfast or dessert — makes about 24

1½ cups all-purpose flour
1 teaspoon baking soda
¼ cup granulated sugar
½ teaspoon salt
¼ cup cocoa

2 eggs
1 cup milk
¼ cup butter or margarine
½ cup milk-chocolate chips

1. Sift the flour, baking soda, sugar, salt, and cocoa into a large bowl.
2. Break the eggs into another bowl (see p. 74). Beat them slightly with a fork, then add the milk and stir.
3. Melt the butter or margarine in a small saucepan over low heat. Set aside to cool.
4. Add the egg mixture to the flour mixture. Mix well.
5. Stir in melted butter or margarine and chocolate chips.
6. Lightly grease a cool griddle and set it on the stove over medium heat.
7. When the griddle is hot enough that a drop of water sizzles on it, spoon the pancake batter, by tablespoonfuls, onto the griddle. Make the pancakes small, about two tablespoons for each pancake.
8. When the tops of the pancakes begin to show air bubbles, flip the pancakes over. Just a minute or two on the second side will be enough.
9. Serve with butter or top with whipped cream or sprinkle with confectioners' sugar.

Mocha Nut Pie

3 squares unsweetened chocolate
2 eggs
¾ cup granulated sugar
¾ cup brown sugar
½ cup butter or margarine
⅔ cup all-purpose flour

¼ teaspoon salt
½ cup milk
2 teaspoons vanilla extract
2 tablespoons instant coffee
1½ cups chopped walnuts

1. Set oven to 350 degrees.
2. Grease a 9-inch pie pan.
3. Drop the chocolate in the top of a double boiler and melt it over hot, **but not boiling**, water. (Stove at lowest setting.) Stir occasionally with a long spoon.
4. When the chocolate is melted, turn off the stove and **carefully** lift off the top of the double boiler. Set chocolate aside to cool.

5. Break the eggs into a small mixing bowl (see p. 74), and beat with an eggbeater until foamy.
6. Mix the granulated sugar, the brown sugar, and the butter or margarine in a large bowl. Beat with a mixing spoon until smooth and creamy.
7. Add the beaten eggs and the cooled chocolate to the sugar mixture. Mix well.
8. Sift the flour and salt into another large bowl.
9. Add *half* the flour mixture to the chocolate mixture. Mix well.
10. Add *half* the milk to the chocolate mixture. Mix.
11. Add the rest of the flour to the chocolate mixture and mix.
12. Add the rest of the milk and mix.
13. Add the vanilla and the coffee. Mix well.
14. Add the nuts and mix.
15. Pour into the prepared pan and bake for 50 to 55 minutes.
16. To serve, top with whipped cream (see p. 11) and nuts.

Dorothy's Banana Chip Muffins

Makes about 24 muffins

⅓ cup butter or margarine
1¾ cups all-purpose flour
½ teaspoon salt
2 tablespoons granulated sugar
2 tablespoons brown sugar
1 tablespoon baking powder

1 egg
¾ cup milk
¾ cup mashed banana (1 average-size banana)
½ cup semi-sweet chocolate chips

1. Set the oven to 400 degrees.
2. Prepare muffin pans by greasing and flouring each cup thoroughly. Or put a paper cupcake liner in each cup.
3. Melt the butter or margarine in a small saucepan over low heat. Set aside to cool.
4. Sift the flour, salt, granulated sugar, brown sugar, and baking powder into a large bowl.
5. Break the egg into another large bowl (see p. 74). Beat with an eggbeater.
6. Add the milk to the beaten egg and stir.
7. Add the mashed banana and the melted butter or margarine to the egg mixture. Mix well.
8. Add the egg mixture to the flour mixture. Mix well, but gently. The batter will be a little lumpy.
9. Add the chocolate chips. Mix gently.
10. Fill each cup in the muffin pan half full. Use a regular cup to pour the batter from the bowl into the cups in the muffin pan.
11. Bake about 20 minutes. Let the muffins cool in the pan for 10 minutes before you remove them to a cake rack.

Ice Cream and Candy

Frozen Chocolate Wonders

Makes 12 pieces of candy

3 squares semi-sweet chocolate
½ teaspoon vanilla extract
1 tablespoon butter or margarine
⅓ cup confectioners' sugar
1 tablespoon cold water

1. Drop the squares of chocolate in the top of a double boiler and melt over hot, **but not boiling,** water. (Stove at lowest setting.) Stir occasionally with a long spoon.
2. When the chocolate is melted, turn off the stove and **carefully** lift off the top of the double boiler. Let the chocolate cool for a few minutes.
3. Add the vanilla and the butter or margarine to the chocolate, and stir.
4. Sift in the confectioners' sugar. Stir well.
5. Add the tablespoon of water and stir.
6. Pour the mixture into a plastic ice cube tray. Cool in the refrigerator for 5 hours.
7. When hard, pop the candy out of the ice cube tray.

When the candy has set for an hour, you can put a toothpick into each square. Then, when the candy has hardened, you have chocolate lollipops.

Spice Balls

Makes about 30 spice balls

½ cup evaporated milk
¼ teaspoon cinnamon
⅛ teaspoon nutmeg
7 or 8 marshmallows
1 cup semi-sweet chocolate chips
⅓ cup raisins

½ cup chopped unsalted nuts
½ cup shredded coconut
1 tablespoon cocoa mixed with 1 tablespoon sugar or — 1 tablespoon instant coffee mixed with 1 tablespoon sugar

1. With a long spoon, mix the evaporated milk, the cinnamon, and the nutmeg in the top of a double boiler.
2. Bring the mixture to a boil.
3. Add the marshmallows and boil for 2 to 3 minutes, stirring constantly.
4. Turn off the stove. Add the chocolate chips, and mix. As soon as the chocolate is blended, **carefully** remove the top of the double boiler.
5. Add the raisins, and mix.
6. Put the top of the double boiler in the refrigerator for about 3 hours, until the mixture hardens enough to be handled.
7. Cover a cookie sheet with waxed paper.
8. Put the nuts, the coconut, and one of the sugar mixtures into separate saucers.
9. When the chocolate mixture is hard enough to handle, drop it, by teaspoonfuls, into either the nuts, the coconut, or the sugar mixture. Wash and dry your hands. Then with your fingers, roll each teaspoonful into a ball.
10. Place the balls on the waxed paper. Put them in the refrigerator or freezer. The colder these are, the better they taste.

Super Rich Chocolate Ice Cream
Makes about 10 servings

1 cup semi-sweet chocolate chips
2 cans sweetened condensed milk (13 ounces each)
1 cup milk
½ teaspoon vanilla extract
½ teaspoon almond extract
2 cups heavy cream (1 pint)

1. Put a large bowl and 2 square 8-inch cake pans in the refrigerator to chill. Also chill the beaters of an electric mixer. Keep the heavy cream in the refrigerator.

2. Melt the chocolate chips in the top of a 2-quart double boiler over hot, **but not boiling,** water.

3. Open the cans of condensed milk and add to the melting chocolate. Cook for 4 minutes, stirring all the time with a long spoon.
4. Add the cup of milk and mix well. Turn off the stove. Let chocolate cool for a minute.
5. Add the vanilla and almond extract and mix in well.
6. When cooled, put the chocolate mixture in the refrigerator, right in the pot it was cooked in.
7. Take the cream, the bowl, and the beater out of the refrigerator. Whip the cream in the bowl (see p. 11).
8. When the cream is stiff and peaky, **fold** (see p. 75) it into the chilled chocolate mixture in the top of the double boiler. Use a large spoon to fold the cream into the chocolate mixture. Work slowly and mix well.
9. Pour the mixture into the chilled pans and put in the freezer part of the refrigerator.
10. About every hour remove the pans, one at a time, and stir the mixture from top to bottom. This will remix the cream, which rises to the top.
11. In about 4 hours the ice cream will be hard enough to serve. For best results, though, leave it in the freezer for 10 hours.

Making Fudge

Fudge is a real treat, but it takes a lot of careful stirring and cooling. If you can make fudge with some friends, you can take turns beating it, and no one will get tired.

Don't be upset if your fudge doesn't thicken properly. You can always put it back in the saucepan and start again. Simply add a tablespoon or two of milk, bring the mixture to a boil and follow the cooking directions again. If the fudge *still* doesn't thicken up enough, you can use it as a lovely, thick, rich sauce over ice cream, cake, or pudding.

Fudge is cooked enough when it reaches the **soft-ball stage.** If you use a candy thermometer, you can stop cooking the fudge when the thermometer, set into the fudge, reaches 235 degrees Fahrenheit. This is the soft-ball stage. Before you put the candy thermometer into the fudge, warm it slightly in a glass of warm water. Then wash it off in warm water before you use it to test the fudge again.

To test for the soft-ball stage without a candy thermometer, drop a bit of the fudge into a cup of cold tap water. If the fudge spreads and mixes easily with the water, it needs to cook longer. But if it stays together and strings down into a blob at the bottom of the cup, test it by pushing the blob into a soft ball with your thumb and forefinger. If the fudge stays in a soft ball, the mixture is done. Let it cool; then beat it. (See directions in recipe.)

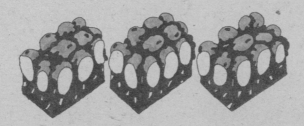

Coconut Walnut Fudge

Makes about 36 pieces

2½ cups granulated sugar
¼ teaspoon salt
2 squares unsweetened chocolate
⅔ cup milk
2 tablespoons light corn syrup

2 tablespoons butter or margarine
1 teaspoon almond extract
½ cup coarsely chopped walnuts
½ cup shredded coconut

1. Grease an 8-inch-square baking pan.
2. Put the sugar, salt, chocolate, milk, and corn syrup into a large saucepan.
3. Cook over low heat, stirring constantly with a long spoon, until the sugar is dissolved.
4. Then, stirring occasionally, keep the mixture boiling over low heat until it reaches the soft-ball stage (see p. 52).
5. Remove the saucepan from the heat and turn off stove. Add the butter or margarine, but do **not** stir it in. Let fudge cool for 10 minutes.
6. When the bottom of the pot is cool enough to touch with your hand, add the extract and beat the fudge with a mixing spoon continually — but not too fast.
7. Stop beating when the fudge is no longer shiny, and when a teaspoonful holds its shape when dropped from the spoon onto the surface of the fudge.
8. Add the nuts and coconut. Stir.
9. Pour the fudge into the prepared pan and cool in the refrigerator for 2 hours.
10. To serve, cut into small squares.

Mocha Fudge

Makes about 36 pieces

2½ cups granulated sugar
½ teaspoon salt
2 squares unsweetened chocolate
¾ cup milk
2 tablespoons light corn syrup
2 tablespoons butter or margarine
1 teaspoon vanilla extract
2 tablespoons instant coffee
½ cup chopped walnuts

○●○●○●○●○

Follow cooking directions for Coconut Walnut Fudge, making sure to add the extract *just* before beating the fudge. Add the instant coffee after step 3. Omit coconut in step 8.

Nutty Marshmallow Fudge

Makes about 36 pieces

2½ cups granulated sugar
¼ teaspoon salt
2 squares unsweetened chocolate
⅔ cup milk
2 tablespoons light corn syrup
2 tablespoons butter or margarine
1 tablespoon vanilla extract
1 cup marshmallow fluff
¾ cup chopped unsalted nuts

○●○●○●○●○

Follow cooking directions for Coconut Walnut Fudge, making sure to add the extract *just* before beating the fudge. Add marshmallow fluff after step 6. Omit coconut in step 8.

Instant Fudge
Makes about 36 pieces

1½ cups granulated sugar
2 tablespoons butter or margarine
½ teaspoon salt
½ cup evaporated milk
2 cups semi-sweet chocolate chips
¾ cup chopped unsalted nuts
1½ teaspoons vanilla extract

1. Grease an 8-inch-square baking pan.
2. With a long spoon, mix the sugar, salt, butter or margarine, and the milk in a large saucepan.
3. Boil the mixture over medium heat for 5 minutes, stirring all the time.
4. Remove the saucepan from the heat, and turn off stove. Add the chocolate chips immediately.
5. Stir until the chocolate melts into mixture.
6. Add the nuts and vanilla. Stir.
7. Pour into the prepared pan and cool in the refrigerator for 2 hours.
8. To serve, cut into small squares.

You can vary this recipe by adding 2 teaspoons of cinnamon in step 2, and substituting ¾ cup of raisins for the nuts in step 6.

Chocolate for Covering Fruits, Nuts, and Marshmallows

Covers at least 2 cups of fruits or nuts, or 24 marshmallows

2 squares unsweetened chocolate
1 cup light corn syrup
¼ cup evaporated milk

½ cup granulated sugar
1 teaspoon vanilla extract

1. Melt the chocolate squares in the top of a double boiler over hot, **but not boiling**, water. (Stove at lowest setting.)
2. Add the corn syrup and the evaporated milk to the melting chocolate. Mix well with a long spoon.
3. Remove the double boiler from the heat. **Carefully** lift off the top of the double boiler and place it directly over the heat.
4. Let chocolate mixture boil slowly over low heat for 15 minutes. Stir occasionally.
5. Add the sugar and boil the chocolate for 5 more minutes.
6. Turn off the stove. Take the pan off the stove. Let cool for a few minutes, then add the vanilla. Mix well.
7. Put the pan in the refrigerator for at least one hour to thicken the chocolate. The longer you have the chocolate in the refrigerator the thicker it will get. But if you leave it there for more than ten hours it will be too hard to work with.
8. Cover a cookie sheet with waxed paper, and assemble the nuts, fruits, and marshmallows for dipping (see next page).

Nuts

Use whole, shelled, unsalted nuts: pecans, walnuts, peanuts, almonds, cashews, filberts, or Brazil nuts.

Use small sugar tongs to dip the nuts into the chocolate. Or drop the nuts — one at a time — into the chocolate and take them out with a *small* spoon.

Put them on the prepared cookie sheet. Put the cookie sheet in the refrigerator, and let the chocolate harden for a few hours.

Marshmallows

Spear the marshmallows with a toothpick and dunk them in the chocolate. For a special treat, dip the marshmallows into a saucer of shredded coconut or crushed nuts before the chocolate hardens.

Put them on the prepared cookie sheet. Put the cookie sheet in the refrigerator, and let the chocolate harden for a few hours.

Fruits

oranges	strawberries	melon
pears	tangerines	cherries
apples	apricots	peaches

Use fresh (not canned) fruits, peeled and cut into chunks. These should be eaten the day you make them.

Pat the chunks of fruit with a paper towel to dry off any water or juice.

Spear the chunks of fruit with a toothpick and dip them into the chocolate.

Put them on the prepared cookie sheet. Put the cookie sheet in the refrigerator, and let the chocolate harden for a few hours.

Puzzles to Eat By

Rhea

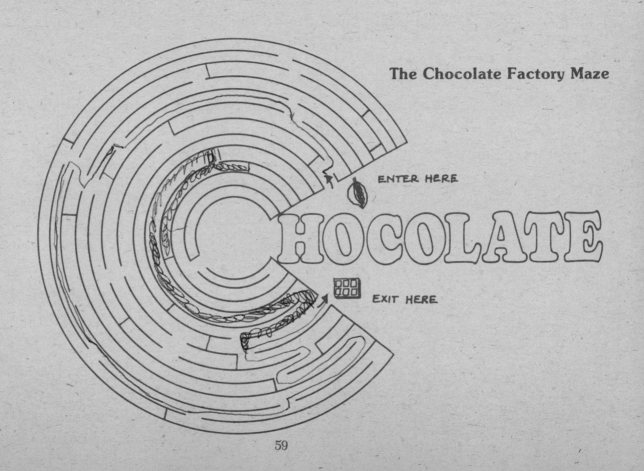

The Chocolate Factory Maze

ENTER HERE

EXIT HERE

Chocolate Rebus Cooking Tips

A rebus puzzle is a sentence in which the words are shown in pictures — as you probably know. To figure out the cooking tips below, write down the letters of each word-picture and add or subtract letters as shown.

TIP #1   M + [belt] – B   [smoke] – IN + [padlock] – PADLK + O + [plate] – P

[ink bottle] – K   A   [door] – OR + [bathtub] – T + [leg] – G

[canoe] + C – [cat] + PILE – P + R

TIP #2   [STOP] + [car] – [acorn] + E   [pit] – P   [fish] – F   A

C + [placemat] – P   [drop] + T – [urn] + Y   [apple] – A + N – [knife] + [ace of spades card]

Get Ready, Set, Cook...

. . . if you can find the list of kitchen tools hidden in this word-find puzzle.
You can look backward, forward, up or down, across, or on the diagonal!

A	R	C	O	O	K	I	E	S	H	O	T	T		~~POT~~
T	E	M	I	K	S	E	R	O	O	M	H	H		PAN
U	O	B	I	N	L	E	N	E	L	D	L	L		DOUBLE BOILER
L	L	P	I	N	C	U	P	L	D	O	P	R		COOKIE SHEET
A	O	C	O	E	L	Z	P	U	P	U	E	R		MIXER
K	H	R	O	V	E	L	O	E	C	B	R	E		MEASURING CUP
N	P	S	F	O	Z	N	N	G	S	L	O	T		SPOON
A	O	P	R	T	K	K	N	I	F	E	V	E		FREEZER
P	T	A	L	S	P	I	F	S	P	B	A	M		KNIFE
E	H	T	E	A	R	R	E	K	N	O	N	O		OVEN
L	O	U	Z	U	E	S	V	S	W	I	R	M		STOVE
E	L	L	S	E	X	P	P	K	H	L	O	R		SPATULA
R	D	A	Z	L	I	A	T	O	P	E	V	E		~~POT HOLDER~~
A	E	E	K	N	M	T	S	A	O	R	E	H		THERMOMETER
M	R	D	A	N	I	E	L	L	E	N	N	T		APRON

61

Chocolate Cookbook Crossword #1

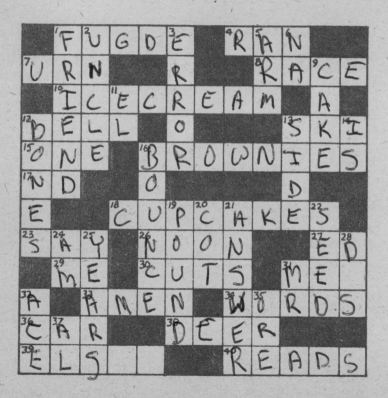

ACROSS

1. Creamy chocolate candy treat.
4. The cocoa spilled and ___ all over the rug.
7. Formal vase or big coffee server.
8. Contest of speed.
10. Frozen chocolate treat.
12. It rings or tolls.
13. Can you ___? (winter sport).
15. Eight minus seven.
16. Chewy, cakelike chocolate squares.
17. North Dakota (abbrev.).
18. Round, frosted, chocolate treats.
23. "O ___ can you see . . ."

26. Midday.
27. Man's nickname.
29. ___, myself, and I.
30. Slices, as cake (verb).
31. Medium or Medical (abbrev.).
33. Word ending a prayer.
34. You find their meanings in a dictionary.
36. Automobile.
38. White-tailed woods animal.
39. Name of a famous cow.
40. A good cook ___ the recipe first.

DOWN
1. Pal.
2. Aunt's husband.
3. Mistake.
5. Your elbow is part of your ___.

6. North America (abbrev.).
9. Chocolate birthday treat.
11. ___ Paso, Texas.
12. Parts of a skeleton.
13. Whose ___ are you on?
14. Opposite of isn't.
16. What a ball does.
19. Sugar is sold by the ___.
20. Small bed.
21. Response to a question.
22. A cacao bean is the ___ of a tree.
24. Morning abbreviation.
25. 100 ___ make one century.
28. Doctor of Dental Surgery (abbrev.).
31. Mister (abbrev.).
32. Highest playing card.
35. Rocks containing iron or other metals.
37. Nickname for Albert.

Candybox Maze

There's one candy left in this amazing candybox — a super delicious chocolate-covered cherry. It's yours if you can get from the entrance to the center of the maze.

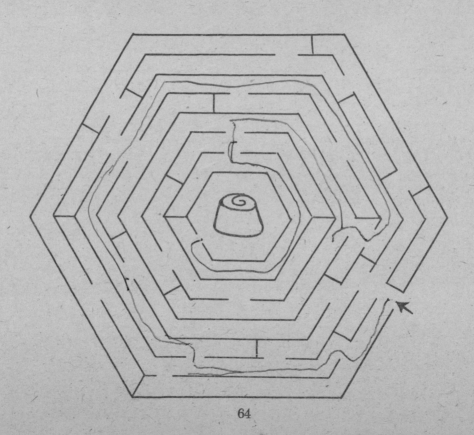

Missing Cookie Ingredients

See if you can find the list of missing cookie ingredients in this word-find puzzle. You can go backward, forward, up or down, across, or on the diagonal.

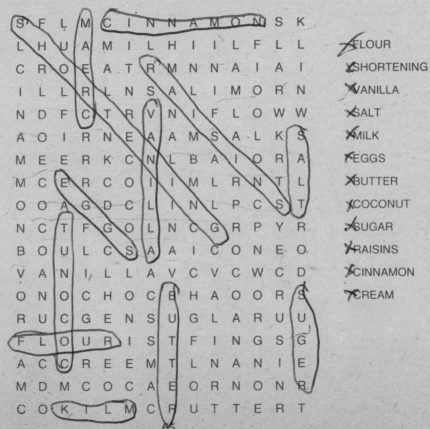

```
S F L M C I N N A M O N S K
L H U A M I L H I I L F L L
C R O E A T R M N N A I A I
I L L R L N S A L I M O R N
N D F C T R V N I F L O W W
A O I R N E A A M S A L K S
M E E R K C N L B A I O R A
M C E R C O I I M L R N T L
O O A G D C L I N L P C S T
N C T F G O L N C G R P Y R
B O U L C S A A I C O N E O
V A N I L L A V C V C W C D
O N O C H O C B H A O O R S
R U C G E N S U G L A R U U
F L O U R I S T F I N G S G
A C C R E E M T L N A N I E
M D M C O C A E O R N O N R
C O K I L M C R U T T E R T
```

- FLOUR
- SHORTENING
- VANILLA
- SALT
- MILK
- EGGS
- BUTTER
- COCONUT
- SUGAR
- RAISINS
- CINNAMON
- CREAM

65

Chocolate Cookbook Crossword #2

ACROSS

2. Name of chocolate bean.
7. Alabama (old abbreviation).
9. Cleaning cloth.
10. You can make either fudge ___ brownies.
12. Wipe your feet on the door ___.
13. A mean fairy tale giant.
15. Man's nickname.
16. Needed to mail a letter.
18. Egg producer.
19. ___ me at school tomorrow.
20. Do re mi ___ so la ti do.
21. European country famous for Alps and milk chocolate.
24. Long, thin, slippery fish.
25. Send him a birthday greeting ___.
26. ___ a cake (create).
27. New Hampshire (abbreviation).

29. Opposite of isn't.
31. We must be sure that no one sees ___.
33. A flying night creature.
35. Taste of unsweetened chocolate.
37. Maine (abbreviation).
38. Necessary for solving a mystery (sing.).
39. Married.
40. Cocoa ___ is the fat in chocolate.

DOWN
1. Checkers is a ___.
2. Mouse's enemy.
3. Explorer who brought cacao beans back to Spain.
4. Either do it ___ else.
5. It happened a long time ___.
6. Center of apple.
8. Young boy.

11. Monthly housing bill.
14. African country that is the biggest supplier of cacao beans.
16. Get ready, get ___, go!
17. He ___ the whole cake!
19. Swiss chocolate is usually ___ chocolate.
20. Place for nose.
21. ___-sweet chocolate is less sweet than most candy.
22. "Pop! Goes the ___."
23. One who dreams.
25. Small cabin.
30. Informal hello.
32. Important part of chair.
34. Nickname for a Kennedy.
35. Furniture for sleeping (sing.).
36. Place for a bath.
39. If you and I both go, ___ can share expenses.

The Identical Birthday Cake Puzzle

Mrs. Goodness ordered identical birthday cakes for her identical twins. The baker put them up on a shelf with a lot of other cakes. Can you help Mrs. Goodness find the two cakes that are exactly alike?

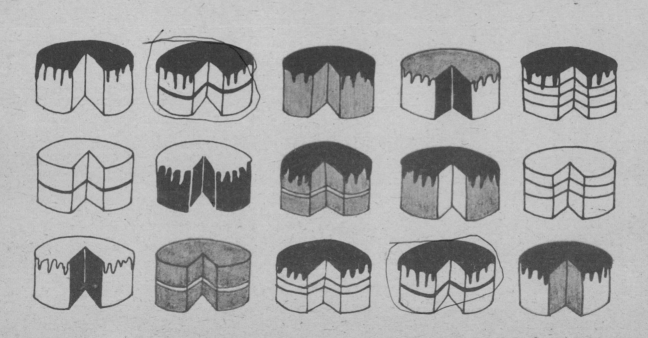

Aw Nuts!

There are eight chocolate-covered nuts in this word-find puzzle. To find them, you can go backward, forward, up or down, across, or on the diagonal.

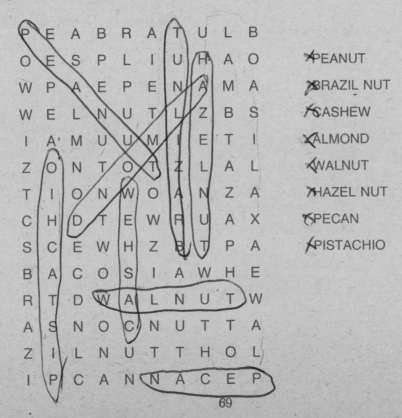

```
P E A B R A T U L B
O E S P L I U H A O
W P A E P E N A M A
W E L N U T L Z B S
I A M U U M I E T I
Z O N T O T Z L A L
T I O N W O A N Z A
C H D T E W R U A X
S C E W H Z B T P A
B A C O S I A W H E
R T D W A L N U T W
A S N O C N U T T A
Z I L N U T T H O L
I P C A N N A C E P
```

PEANUT

BRAZIL NUT

CASHEW

ALMOND

WALNUT

HAZEL NUT

PECAN

PISTACHIO

69

Chocolate Words

Using only the letters C-H-O-C-O-L-A-T-E, can you spell out words that fit the clues below? In each word you make, you can repeat C and O only, since both letters are used twice in CHOCOLATE.

1. The opposite of *warm* (not cold): __ __ __ __.

2. The name of the bean from which chocolate is made:

   __ __ __ __ __.

3. A person who supervises a team:

   __ __ __ __ __.

4. Rain or suit __ __ __ __.

5. Opposite of love: __ __ __ __.

6. What the person in charge of a class does:

   __ __ __ __ __.

7. The sound an owl makes is called a __ __ __ __.

8. To be dishonest in a game is to __ __ __ __ __.

9. Center of a doughnut: __ __ __ __.

10. Medicine helps a wound to __ __ __ __.

11. A story like "Cinderella" is a fairy __ __ __ __.

12. Hammer, screwdriver, or saw: __ __ __ __.

13. A favorite soda pop flavor: __ __ __ __.

14. What fire makes: __ __ __ __.

15. Baseball players wear gloves to help them __ __ __ __ __.

16. Opposite of early: __ __ __ __.

17. Part of the foot: __ __ __.

18. Place where travelers stay: __ __ __ __ __.

19. Friendly, informal talk: __ __ __ __.

20. Favorite chocolate drink: __ __ __ __ __.

21. Young horse: __ __ __ __.

22. It makes heat: __ __ __ __.

Safety and Cooking Tips

1. **Before you cook**
   - Choose a time to cook when the kitchen is free.
   - Put on an apron and tie back long hair.
   - Read through the recipe to be sure you have all the ingredients and equipment before you start.
   - Get out all the things you will need.
   - If you are baking, have an adult light the oven.

2. **Adults present:** In addition to helping you when you use the oven and stove, an adult *must* help you in using knives, choppers, blenders, and mixers. In fact, it is a good idea to have an adult nearby while you are cooking, in case of emergency.

3. **Use potholders** when taking pans and cookie sheets out of the oven, or in lifting saucepans off the stove. Place hot pans on wood or metal surfaces — where they can't melt, crack, or damage anything. Don't rush when removing pans or saucepans. Accidents can burn — *you*.

4. **If your oven** has a thermostat and timer, use them. It is best to stay in the kitchen until you finish cooking. With these recipes, don't ever leave saucepans unwatched when they are on direct heat.

5. **Preparing ingredients and pans**

• **Chocolate:** Unless chocolate chips or cocoa are named, the chocolate called for is hard, bitter, cooking chocolate. This must be melted — but not over direct heat! If you don't have a double boiler, put the chocolate in a small saucepan set in a larger saucepan ¼ to ⅓ full of very hot water. There are pre-melted unsweetened chocolates (Baker's Redi-Blend is one) that you can use in place of hard unsweetened chocolate. Be sure to read the information on the pre-melted chocolate packet before you use it.

• **Dry ingredients:** Use a sieve or sifter (not a colander) to sift dry ingredients (flour, salt, baking powder, spice) together into your mixtures. (Sugar is dry, but is added separately, usually first.)

• **Eggs**

How to break an egg: Hold egg over bowl and *tap* side of egg with edge of knife to crack the shell. Using two hands, pull halves apart and let egg plop into bowl.

Separating egg yolks from whites: If yolks and whites are to be used separately, flop the yolk from one half shell to the other above a bowl, until most of the white is collected in the bowl. Then plop the yolk into another bowl.

Beating egg whites: Use a dry bowl and beater. Eggs should be at room temperature. Beat at highest speed until whites are really stiff. When the beater is pulled out they should form stiff peaks.

• **Shortening (grease):** Margarine can usually be substituted for butter unless a recipe says to use only butter. When just shortening is called for, use canned, solid white shortening like Crisco. Soften shortening before using by letting it warm up in the room. Don't melt it unless called for.

• **Sugar:** Granulated sugar (table sugar) is used for cooking and baking. Confectioners' sugar is powdered sugar, and is used in frostings and whipped cream.

6. **Greasing pans:** Dip a piece of paper towel into shortening and smear it thinly all over the inside of a cool pan. If the recipe says to also flour the pan, shake a handful of flour into the greased pan and tilt the pan this way and that until the entire greased area is thinly coated with flour.

7. **Pouring batter:** Tilt the mixing bowl over the pan and scoop out batter with a large spoon. Or, if bowl is heavy, dip out batter with a ladle or cup, then scrape out the last of the batter with a spoon.

8. **Folding:** To fold egg whites or whipped cream into a mixture, first pour them on top of mixture. Then bring your spoon down through the mixture and up again. Keep mixing gently in a circle from top to bottom until thoroughly blended. (Do not beat or you will spoil the foamy, airy consistency.)

9. **Testing for doneness:** To see if cakes are done, first open oven door completely. Pull out oven rack a little way, using a potholder, and pull cake pan toward you, using a potholder. To test, push a toothpick straight down into the center of the cake, and pull it out. If it is clean, the cake is done. You can also press the center of the cake lightly (and fast) with your finger. If the cake doesn't dent but bounces back, it's done.

   Cookies are done when they feel firm to a light touch. If you find they aren't done when you have taken them out, you can always put them back in the oven for a few minutes.

10. **Cooling and removing cakes from pans:** Let cakes stand for 10 minutes after taking them from oven. Run the flat side of a knife around the sides of the cake. Then put cake rack on top of pan, and, holding both rack and pan firmly, turn over the rack and pan. Set the rack on a flat surface and remove pan. If you need to get the top side of the cake face up, simply repeat the turnover process. Let the cake cool thoroughly and move it to a plate before you frost it.

Cookies: Let cookies cool for 5 to 10 minutes after removing from oven. Then carefully, with a spatula, lift them one by one onto a plate. Let them thoroughly cool before you store them in a cookie jar. If you use a cookie sheet over and over — as you will if you are making a big batch of cookies at one time — be sure to grease the sheet again, before you put the next batch of cookie batter on it.

11. **After you cook**
    - Put away all ingredients, making sure caps on bottles and covers on jars are screwed on firmly.
    - Store syrups or sauces in the refrigerator. Store solid chocolate in a cool (not cold) dry place.
    - Wash your pans and utensils and straighten up the kitchen so that you can return another day to make another great chocolate treat.

Answers

Page 59 *The Chocolate Factory Maze*

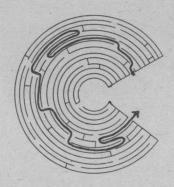

Page 60 *Chocolate Rebus Cooking Tips*
#1 Melt chocolate in a double boiler.
#2 Store it in a cool dry place.

Page 61 *Get Ready, Set, Cook!*

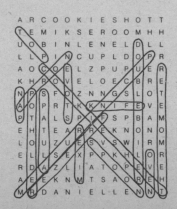

Page 62 *Chocolate Cookbook Crossword #1*

Page 64 *Candybox Maze*

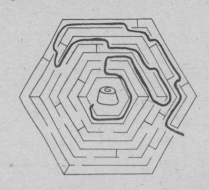

Page 65 *Missing Cookie Ingredients*

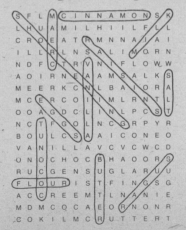

Page 66 *Chocolate Cookbook Crossword #2*

Page 68   *The Identical Birthday Cake Puzzle*

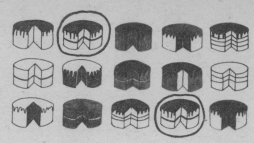

Page 69   *Aw Nuts!*

Page 70   *Chocolate Words*

   1. cool   2. cacao   3. coach   4. coat   5. hate

   6. teach   7. hoot   8. cheat   9. hole   10. heal

  11. tale   12. tool   13. cola   14. heat   15. catch

  16. late   17. toe   18. hotel   19. chat   20. cocoa

  21. colt   22. coal